BURMA'S FAMILY TREE

ALBERT
-COBURG
-OTHA
1861

Helena
-1923
n
aristian of
-Holstein
-1917
ldren)

Princess Louise
1849-1939
m
John, 9th Duke of Argyll
1845-1915

Prince Arthur
Duke of Connaught
1850-1942
m
Princess Louise Margaret
of Prussia
1860-1917
(3 children)

Prince Leopold
Duke of Albany
1853-1884
m
Princess Helen of Waldeck
1861-1922
(2 children)

Princess Beatrice
1857-1944
m
Prince Henry
of Battenberg
1858-1896

Duke
Louis
sse
1937

Eleonore
ch
937

Princess Alice of Hesse
1872-1918
m
Tsar Nicholas II of Russia
1868-1918
(5 children)

2 others

Alexander
1st Marquess of Carisbrooke
1886-1960
m
Lady Irene Denison
1890-1956

Princess Victoria Eugenie
(Ena) of Battenberg
1887-1969
m
King Alfonso III of Spain
1886-1941

Lord Leopold
Mountbatten
1889-1922

Prince Maurice
of Battenberg
1891-1914

uess
Haven
38

Nada
y
63

LOUIS,
EARL MOUNTBATTEN
OF BURMA
1900-1979
m
EDWINA ASHLEY
1901-1960

Grand Duke
George Donatus
1906-1937
m
Princess Cecile
of Greece
1911-1937
(3 children)

Prince Louis
1908-1968
m
Margaret Geddes
1913-

Lady Iris
Mountbatten
1920-
m
Michael Bryan
(1 child)

Don Jaime
Duke of Segovia
1908-
m
Countess Emmanuele
de Dampierre
(2 children)

Don Juan
Count of Barcelona
1913-
m
Infanta Maria of Spain
1910-

3 others

Philip
Edinburgh
21-
n
Elizabeth
26-
Queen
beth II)

Lady Tatiana
Mountbatten
1917-

David, 3rd Marquess
of Milford Haven
1919-1970
m
Janet Bryce
1932-

Lady Patricia
Mountbatten
Countess Mountbatten of Burma
1924-
m
Lord Brabourne
1924-

Lady Pamela
Mountbatten
1929-
m
David Hicks
1929-

Don Juan Carlos
King of Spain
1938-
m
Princess Sophie of Greece
1938-
(3 children)

3 others

Lady
Knatchbull
955-
m
n Hubert
Breuil
956-

Lady
Amanda Knatchbull
1957-

Hon.
Philip Knatchbull
1961-

Hon.
Nicholas Knatchbull
1964-1979

Hon.
Timothy Knatchbull
1964-

Edwina Hicks
1961-
m
Jeremy Brudenell
1960-

Ashley Hicks
1963-

India Hicks
1967-

INDIA HICKS

A SLICE OF ENGLAND

INDIA HICKS

A SLICE OF ENGLAND

Photography by Miguel Flores-Vianna
Foreword by Carolina Herrera

RIZZOLI
NEW YORK
New York · Paris · London · Milan

To my exceptional mother

PARKINSON

Folio
Name

TABLE OF CONTENTS

FOREWORD BY CAROLINA HERRERA 11

INTRODUCTION 13

PART 1 LEGACY

A STORIED LIFE 17

BRITWELL HOUSE 33

THE GROVE 51

VIEWS & VISTAS 91

PART 2 THE NEW TRADITION

AMERICA FARM 115

Upstairs 116
Downstairs 139

MARMITE & MINCE PIES 179

COUNTRY LIFE 195

POSTSCRIPT 219

ACKNOWLEDGMENTS 220

CREDITS 224

FOREWORD

BY CAROLINA HERRERA

I have always been interested in the origins of taste. In this book, you will find—beautifully illustrated—the stupendous genealogy of India Hicks's style and taste. To some extent, we are all influenced by our background and childhood—what we have seen and been affected by. India is well known for her exotic and wonderful family life that she leads on an enchanting island in the West Indies. It is always a pleasure to visit India and see the wonderful mixture that she has created in her house, where style, comfort, a touch of royalty, and lots of humor live happily together.

In both charming photographs and anecdotes, she gives us a glimpse of Broadlands, the house of her impossibly glamorous grandparents, Lord Louis and Lady Edwina Mountbatten. She also shares the house that she grew up in, Britwell in Oxfordshire, which was the creation of her father, David Hicks, one of the great interior designers of the last century.

India's new house in England is close to home both in its location and in the placement of family furniture and inherited objects. It features her contemporary touches, her sense of humor, and the energy of her young family, and it is a place where grand consoles and mirrors rub shoulders with mounted bathing caps in Lucite display cases and Pop Art sits by a Georgian desk.

These houses echo tradition and taste and a sense of order and Englishness, but there is something else on every page…a sense of fun.

INTRODUCTION

This book is the story of four English houses.

I thought at first it would simply be the lurching journey of bringing our new English country house, America Farm, to life: the architectural choices, the planning challenges, the compromises and concessions my partner, David, and I made along the way, even before we dared to think about where to place the loo roll.

However, I soon recognized that so much of what had informed our decisions had been drawn from the past and, particularly for me, from the three houses in which I had spent my childhood: Broadlands, Britwell, and the Grove.

The past is always the place to start for inspiration. Its textures, tastes, and visions are what shape us. In revisitation and remembrance, we bring back that which is not always fresh in the mind but always familiar to the heart.

PART 1

LEGACY

A STORIED LIFE

I always think that my mother must have the second-best design eye in England. How could she not? From birth, she was surrounded by dazzling people, places, houses, and history, and then she married the great master of design, who had the number-one eye. But perhaps I'm biased—they are my parents, after all.

For the most part, my mother's life has been lived deep in the English countryside. Her parents' home, Broadlands, was a stately English home set amongst six thousand acres of Hampshire land.

A fine example of mid-Georgian architecture, Broadlands stands serenely with a unique place in British history. Its owners and many of its distinguished visitors have helped to shape the course of history. To me as a young child, it was simply my grandfather's home. We would spend each Christmas there and stay every summer during the Romsey Horse Show, with odd weekends peppered in between.

My earliest memories are of running through the vast front door, into the pale blue octagonal domed hall, under the decorative-plaster ceiling, through the rounded arch, and into the sculpture hall, where Father Christmas, in his somewhat suspicious farm boots, would welcome us on Christmas Eve, smelling slightly of cow's milk.

The sculpture hall displays pieces of Greek and Roman works acquired in 1765 by the 2nd Viscount Palmerston during an obligatory Grand Tour, which of course completed the education of any young English aristocrat. It was a far cry from what I did, which was puttering around the world with a backpack and a Walkman listening to Spandau Ballet. My mother's childhood did not entail listening to Spandau Ballet, but to Sir Malcolm Sargent, a close friend of my grandparents who would frequently entertain the family and guests with impromptu piano recitals.

PAGE 4: My mother, with her much-recognized David Hicks–designed hairdo. PAGES 6-7: The Portland stone fireplace at America Farm, custom made by us with Jamb in London. PAGE 8: Assorted memorabilia inside the gothic cabinets my father designed. PAGE 10: A slightly impractical chair, upholstered by my father in purple leather. As children, we were never ever allowed to sit on them—obviously. PAGE 12: Rather stern-looking relatives watch the comings and goings at America Farm. PAGE 14: My grandfather, as Colonel-in-Chief of the Life Guards, in the courtyard of Buckingham Palace. Because of that hefty silver breastplate, he could not bend down. I remember being lifted up in order to kiss him when he was in ceremonial dress. PAGE 16: My grandfather dressed as Admiral of the Fleet (foreground photograph) and wearing the Star of India satin robe, adorned with the orders and decorations that he been awarded, with my grandmother beside him (background photograph). ABOVE: The riverfront to Broadlands, showing off the portico. OPPOSITE: Painted illustrations of Broadlands hang on my mother's cupboard, which houses an impressive amount of handbags.

Broadlands

To India from Grandpapa

OPPOSITE: You can tell that my grandfather was a naval top dog because of all those gold-braid rings. The spaghetti-looking bits on his shoulder are called aiguillettes and are derived from a rope and stick one would use to tether his horse in the ground. ABOVE: A button from the staff uniform worn by his footman.

The drawing room is not only impressive because of its furnishings, objets d'art, and superbly intricate ceiling, but also because of its collection of eighteenth- and nineteenth-century British portraits, including ones by Sir Joshua Reynolds, George Romney, and Sir Henry Raeburn.

I recall being brought down for tea in the Wedgwood room, smartly dressed and on my best behavior. In this room, Classical friezes and moldings are reminiscent of Josiah Wedgwood's pottery decoration. The plasterwork incorporates original 1790 oval looking mirrors, and the two built-in pediment bookcases house a collection of eighteenth-century French plays and literature. During World War II, when Broadlands became a hospital annex, this room was used as a ward, and patients could gaze up at the magnificent ceilings while lying in bed.

One year, my grandfather was invited to the Wedgwood factory and took his younger grandchildren with him. His face, as a recognized man of action in world affairs, was to be immortalized on a small Wedgwood dish. We children were allowed to try our hands at creating one of these. My brother's was done to perfection, our grandfather's profile in white placed perfectly centered on the blue pottery; mine was placed haphazardly, with my grandfather's nose pointing further south than he would have liked.

In the library, we would gather every Christmas around a small crackling television set to watch the Queen's Speech, sitting among the two walls lined with bookcases and a display of swords and daggers given to my grandfather, including a macabre headhunter's sword, presented by Naga tribesmen at Shillong, India, the hilt of which was decorated with human hair.

Walking past the Oak Room and up the great north staircase would take you to the Portico Room, which had curtains, a sofa, and a four-poster bed covered in an informal chintz. Whenever we crept into this room, we would stare at this fabric, searching for the delicately traced profile of a young Queen Victoria and her Prince Consort, as this chintz was originally ordered for the royal yacht in 1854. It was oddly appropriate that the current Queen slept here on her honeymoon.

The Chinese Room is decorated in a vividly colored modern paper selected by the late King of Sweden in 1956, but hidden behind a panel above the fireplace is the original Chinese wall paper, preserved from 1769.

The Green Room takes its name from its color scheme and has a huge canopied green-and-white four-poster bed and a collection of pictures by Philip de László.

And I bet you can't guess why the Palmerston Room is called the Palmerston Room. This was Lord Palmerston's bedroom. He was a warmhearted handsome character who, like his father, inherited Broadlands at age seventeen and became not only foreign minister but also prime minister. A countryman at heart, he would often ride eighty miles from London to Broadlands on horseback.

OPPOSITE: Any more achievements, titles, or decorations, and my grandfather would have needed an extension to his passport.

ADMIRAL OF THE FLEET
THE RIGHT HONOURABLE
EARL MOUNTBATTEN OF BURMA.
K.G., P.C., G.C.B., G.C.S.I. G.C.I.E, G.C.V.O.,
D.S.O.
BRITISH PASSPORT
DIEU ET MON DROIT
UNITED KINGDOM OF GREAT BRITAIN
AND NORTHERN IRELAND
394806

OPPOSITE: The dining room at Broadlands was brought brightly from the 1920s into the 1980s when my father was invited to redecorate it. The family was quite startled at the result. ABOVE: The Wedgwood room, with the table laid for afternoon tea and a lot of pieces of Wedgwood china dotted about the space. Do note the silver kettle, for hot water with the flame underneath, then a teapot for China tea and another for Indian tea.

ABOVE: My grandmother's scalloped pillowcase with her EM initials. There were, of course, matching sheets, made in Paris by D. Porthault. OPPOSITE: Always have your crest embroidered inside your fur—it's very useful for identification.

IN HONOUR BOUND
LORD LOUIS MOUNTBATTEN
HONI SOIT QUI MAL Y PENSE

After Lord Palmerston's death, two days before his eighty-first birthday and while he was still serving as prime minister, the house passed to his stepson, then onto my grandmother's grandfather, and finally to my grandmother.

Despite the beauty of the inside of the house, my mother always says that it was the outside that captured her imagination. The house stands on a slightly raised terrace with views westward over lawns to parkland and beyond. The River Test flows by, seen from the front lawn and through the magical gardens that had been shaped by Capability Brown in the eighteenth century for the 1st Lord Palmerston. Just below the drawing room, the river curves majestically around a gigantic Spanish chestnut tree.

After my grandmother inherited Broadlands, she decided to knock down the Victorian bachelor wing that conflicted with the classical look of the main house. It was full of nasty little rooms and considered much too ugly and expensive to keep up. Work began to demolish it. One night my grandmother, recently returned from a trip overseas, woke from a dream too terrified to look out the window. She had dreamt about a conversation with one of the workmen, who had said, "We've done a lot whilst you were away and do hope you'll be pleased. We have straightened up that river."

On the grounds there was an ornamental dairy, designed for the delight of the Palmerston ladies and their guests, who would have fun playing at milking and making butter. There was a walled garden, which protected three other gardens. The first had apple tunnels and a greenhouse, and the walls themselves were covered in espaliered plum trees and mulberry trees planted by King James I.

In the next was a flower-and-vegetable garden, beyond that a white garden, and below all three a tranquil Japanese garden with a decorative bridge and a summerhouse over a pool.

There was also a glass orangery in which orange and lemon trees grew among camellia and gardenia. Can you imagine the fragrance? The 3rd Lord Palmerston, Queen Victoria's prime minister, had held parliamentary meetings in it nearly a hundred years before.

During World War II, my mother and her sister were evacuated from London and sent to stay with Mrs. Cornelius Vanderbilt at 640 Fifth Avenue in New York City. Some years later I was visiting the Metropolitan Museum of Art with my mother, and she said "Ah, very familiar" as we passed by a huge malachite vase, taller than my nine-year-old daughter, Domino. "That was in the cavernous hallway of Mrs. Vanderbilt's city home," she explained. Of course, my mother also spent time in Mrs. Vanderbilt's residence on Bellevue Avenue in Newport, Rhode Island. That was not a small house either.

OPPOSITE: My grandfather's rather exuberant bookplate and other crests, which would have been worn by the Indian footmen on their chests during the time my grandfather was Viceroy of India. Contrary to what you might expect, the grander servants would have had a brass badge pinned on their uniforms; the lesser-ranking ones would have had it embroidered on.

When my mother returned from America, Broadlands had been transformed into a hospital, and it was humming with ambulances and nurses buzzing about in starched white uniforms. My grandmother, only recently adjusting to these arrangements herself, had certainly had time to register a newly erected little wooden building set between two porticoes. This apparently was where all the bedpans were to be emptied, just in sight of the drawing room.

My mother recalls that one of the many visitors to Broadlands during this time was General Eisenhower. My grandfather was particularly anxious to make a good impression on the great man, especially as he was Supreme Allied Commander in Europe and outranked my grandfather, who was only Chief of Combined Operations. So it was with alarm that my grandparents and mother watched Eisenhower's huge Cadillac navigate the narrow cattle grid and eventually veer off the driveway and into a ditch.

Another famous guest was Irving Berlin, who was in Britain to entertain the troops, and he accompanied some of the soldiers to Broadlands. My mother's grandmother was delighted to meet him, as her husband had been to a restaurant in New York when Irving Berlin was a singing waiter.

Even more Americans were billeted to Broadlands, living at the end of the drive when another of the houses on the estate was given over. My grandparents would invite the officers in, as they were fascinated to see the interiors of Broadlands. My mother, only twelve years old at the time, would give guided tours. When asked who had painted the eighteenth-century panels depicting classical scenes on the ceiling of the drawing room, she answered, "Helena Rubinstein." The response was electric—"Say, is that so? We had no idea she did this kind of thing!" exclaimed the surprised audience—and that was the moment my mother realized her mistake. However, she was too embarrassed to say that the paintings were, in fact, done by the ubiquitous artist Angelica Kauffmann and not the queen of cosmetics.

Although my grandmother had the American decorator Nell Cosden work on her London home, Brook House, Broadlands was largely left untouched until my father got his hands on it many, many years later. After the war, when the house once again reverted from hospital to home, the King of Sweden, my grandfather's brother-in-law, had great fun with my grandmother rearranging the very valuable lapis lazuli and antique china collections brought back out from storage.

My mother also remembers fierce games of cards being played on folding card tables. Whenever the King of Sweden would whisper to himself, "Oh how appropriate" as he picked a certain card, they knew he was holding a king.

But my mother and aunt were always rather alarmed when they played against him and his sister-in-law, Princess Alice, Prince Philip's mother, as he would mutter, "Stupid old fool" at her when she played her cards badly. It was particularly jarring, as she would be dressed in her nun's habit.

As a child, my mother mainly lived on the nursery floor, at the end of which was a sizable room that held two large desks for her and her sister. My mother never remembers being taught at these desks—the room was more a sitting room for them. I, on the other hand, remember this room well, as I was made to sit in here and revise my multiplication tables with my nanny over Christmas holidays spent at Broadlands every year. (I still don't really know anything beyond the sevens times table.)

Christmas at Broadlands was very traditional. A huge tree cut from the estate would be towering in the marble hallway. As children we would hang up our stockings waiting to be filled by Father Christmas, the biggest and therefore most popular stockings happened to be my grandfather's shooting socks. An impressively long polished mahogany dining table would be lavishly laid up and uniformed footmen would serve turkey, bread sauce, and stuffing. I would have sneaked into the pantry corridor beside the dining room before lunch, when most of the adults were out shooting, leaving Nanny anxiously searching for me upstairs while I stole handfuls of the Quality Street sweets from an unguarded tin.

There was much to look forward to on visits to my grandfather—seeing my beloved cousins, being able to ride one of his horses for hours across endless farm land (not once having to dismount to open an interfering gate), gazing into the glass cases of my grandfather's model ships, and being allowed to stay up past my bedtime and sit in his cinema with oversized seats and fiddle with the metal ashtrays in the arms. What I remember most, however, is the excitement of riding in the elevator, standing on tip toes to push the big round buttons. I can still remember the feeling of that elevator landing with a gentle thump, the doors slowly and carefully opening onto another floor, with a mass of other rooms, home to many more inherited treasures.

BRITWELL HOUSE

"What do your fathers do?" I remember the teacher asking the classroom of children. Other fathers were lawyers, farmers, or bank managers. Mine was an interior decorator, and this was always met with an awkward silence because no one, including me, really knew what it meant. Did other fathers design their mother's hairdo or their own dancing shoes or their funeral? I suspected the other children did not live in a 1728 mansion that was used as a design laboratory, nor did they holiday in a house inspired by an Egyptian mausoleum or have golden pheasants and peacocks as pets.

Having David Hicks as my father was anything but dull. I assumed that everyone lived in a world of vibrating color, where walls of pink felt met purple tweed cushions, clashing with vermillion carpets and maroon-upholstered furniture.

My parents married on a snowy day in Hampshire in 1960. It was so cold and full of snow that Noël Coward said, "This is carrying decorating too far!"

My father was a keen shot, a keen horseman, and—surprisingly—a devoted countryman. He, like my mother, lived most of his life in the English countryside.

His was, and remains to this day, a name to reckon with. He made a statement. Unlike many other designers, you can tell a Hicks room when you see it. He mixed yesterday with today before anybody else did. Who else had thought to place a Louis XV commode in a modern room?

My father was completely confident in his use of color and pattern. He had a fearless relationship with pink, scarlet, and orange. He woke up the quiet drawing rooms of England, blew away the cobwebs, and let the world know about it. His creations tended to be on a grand scale: a villa above Monte Carlo for Robert de Balkany, the original nightclub aboard the Queen Elizabeth 2, a private suite for the Prince of Wales at Buckingham Place, and the home of Vidal Sassoon.

OPPOSITE: Britwell House as seen from the top of Britwell Hill, which I was always considered too young to bicycle down, unlike my older brother and sister, who were allowed to enjoy this thrill. I have never moved past this.

He was a voracious explorer, discovering architectural wonders and surprises. He never once thought that a gate marked private actually meant private, and he would take us, as children, on grand tours around Europe. My brother paid full attention, while my sister and I dreamt of ponies.

Nothing was impossible if he wanted something done in life; immediate action normally followed.

When his driver's license was taken away, in his late sixties, he would drive across fields—some his own, some belonging to neighbors—and walk the last half mile in order to make the Sunday-morning service. He was prone to exquisite snobberies, which were liable to sudden changes. In his final days, he suffered a small heart attack and my mother called an ambulance. When it arrived, my father refused to get in—he would not be driven in such a common vehicle and insisted my mother drive him to the hospital herself.

My father believed all design required intense enthusiasm, style, and understanding, and his spirit for and awareness of design never stopped, not even for lunch. He complained that Sunday lunch had no style to it at all. "I like inventive cooking," he would say every Sunday when faced with the traditional roast.

OPPOSITE: The black canal, which was placed there by my father as a little embellishment to the garden's view of the house. ABOVE: The front of Britwell showing one of the two wings.

PAGE 36: The trough where we would stop for the horses to drink after my mother and I rode miles across the Chiltern Hills. PAGE 37: The black canal as it is today. My father would not approve of the water lilies. PAGES 38–39: The obelisk, erected in 1778 by the first owner of the house, with a Latin inscription in memory of his parents. OPPOSITE: The allée my father planted knowing that his children's children's children would grow up enjoying this vista. Then the house got sold. Somewhat of a surprise. ABOVE: The inscription and H logo my father added to the obelisk when they bought the house.

PAGE 42: The hall at Britwell, with the bowler hats my father wore riding. A top hat would have been worn for hunting. In the corner is a banana tree in a basket, an expensive experiment in the English countryside. PAGE 43: The dining room, converted from the original chapel; real candles burn in the chandelier. Under the starched white tablecloth is red damask that matches the painted walls and thick curtains. PAGE 44: My mother's bedroom in an abundance of green David Hicks Z fabric and an H-logo white bedspread. PAGE 45: Not your average bathroom! My father always liked to place the tub in the middle of the room to add some drama. ABOVE: The drawing room in its first incarnation. The modern painting concerned my grandfather, who thought it looked like childbirth.

He paid great attention to lighting and thought not so much in terms of color, but in terms of color schemes. He believed that the quality of furniture and objects in a room were less important than the manner in which they were put together. And he did not mind mixing styles from different periods, holding that good design always goes with good design.

He was sharp, witty, and irreverent, and what he brought to design was an impeccable eye coupled with a dominant personality. He made full use of both in his dealings with his clients, and at his peak he oversaw a global empire of shops and franchises.

My parents bought Britwell House just after they married. My father had seen it advertised in the *Times*, but my mother was already familiar with the estate, as her childhood friend had once lived in one of the wings and boasted about it being the best countryside for riding. My grandfather was horrified by the purchase and told my newlywed parents that it was much too large for them and they would never be able to fill it. My father quickly proved that wrong: it might have taken two years to decorate, but the house was filled almost immediately.

Raine Spencer (Princess Diana's stepmother) was visiting once and pushed the bell beside her bed to summon the maid, Pat. Pat arrived promptly with a "Yes, milady?" Raine said, "I do wish you could silence that peacock for me. Can you see what you can do?" The peacocks were a happy pair called Perseus and Ariadne, and they eventually had to be given away because they were rather noisy—but not before they gave birth to a baby, known only as the Egg. The Egg grew up to be a handsome peacock who screamed as much as his parents, and so all three found a new family to live with, a nice couple with a large garden. Unfortunately, they kept flying back to Britwell.

Although we only lived there until I was twelve, I remember certain things about Britwell very clearly. On the top floor was a long nursery landing, at the end of which was a swing. The nursery itself had a semicircular attic window, over which was hung curtains made of white chintz, lined and edged with dark cedar green. Can you imagine, white chintz in a children's room?

My parents' bathrooms were separated across a hallway. My father's was carpeted in one of his own designs in brown, cream, and black, which was inspired by a Persian mosaic. The striped curtains were putty black–and-white cotton, and there was a Victorian weighing machine that belonged to my grandfather and a Regency Gothic gilt library chair. Yes, there was a leather library chair in the bathroom. A studded screen hid the loo, and black and white–paneled walls produced the effect of a sitting room.

My mother's bathroom, on the other hand, was light and airy. It had a central bath with a huge chandelier hanging over it, an elaborate English cabinet, and two red armchairs designed by Lord Snowdon for the Prince of Wales's investiture in 1969. I have always found this amusing—like goody bags at a children's party, you were allowed to take home the chairs you sat on during the ceremony.

I used to creep into my mother's bedroom at night, which had white paneling and white tweed curtains with bright yellow shantung edging. The pelmet was inspired by those in an early eighteenth-century Swedish castle. When my little feet walked across her emerald-green carpet, I could feel the raised white motif. On special occasions I would be allowed to climb into the bergère upholstered in brilliant yellow to sit at her dressing table, which was draped in a rich peacock-blue fabric. The dachshunds' wicker basket, with matching yellow cushion, was always in the corner.

ABOVE: My father was delighted to find that Britwell came with an octagonal room; to emphasize this further, he added an octagonal rug of his own design. On top of the table struts an elaborate wooden peacock.

Because children were only to be seen and certainly not heard, I never spent much time in the drawing room, but the image I see posted the most on Instagram is of this room. The space had startling pale apple-green sofas, which were set on either side of the 1760s carved wood–and-marble fireplace, above which hung a modern abstract painting, and beside which was a Louis XVI chair covered in a very dark coral silk velvet. When was the last time you thought about dark coral and apple green sitting beside each other?

Any guest arriving for a country weekend would be welcomed by the butler in the 1728 entrance hall, which had a large fireplace reminiscent of Vanbrugh, a black-and-white stone floor, and a gigantic log basket. The guest would then be invited upstairs to his or her bedroom, passing the bold blue-and-white patterned wallpaper on the staircase, which my father had adapted from a fragment of Portuguese woven linen.

There was an Octagon Room, quite literally in the shape of an octagon, where drinks were poured; a dining room with a magnificent domed plasterwork ceiling, originally built as a Catholic chapel; a breakfast room with an endlessly long pine table; a library with a red-lacquered television set and a gray flannel sofa; and my mother's study, where they installed the panels originally painted in 1937 by Rex Whistler for the London boudoir of my grandmother, Edwina Mountbatten. Removed when World War II broke out, they were stored in Broadlands for safekeeping. Pretty lucky really since a German bomb dropped directly through that London room a few weeks later.

For the most part, Britwell was a well-lived-in, comfortable, perfectly designed example of an eighteenth-century English country house, apart from the Long Room, a very modern space my father conceived with walls of pink felt and vibrating scarlets, purples, and puces. "Those are not colors for the daytime," my mother would say. Indeed, it was a nighttime room where my father stayed up late and listened to music at a loud volume. The whole space was somewhat astonishing for the English countryside.

In decorating and indeed all aspects of his life, my father was a traditionalist with a wicked twist. Instead of a predictable overcoat, he wore a long, black cape. It had a scarlet lining that would float out behind him as he strode about, and underneath it was a blazer in bottle green instead of the more usual navy. He would travel on business trips to Tokyo or New York with flowers in bud, cut from his greenhouse and wrapped in plastic.

He designed absolutely everything around him—once even the nose of a client. The only thing he did not design was his H logo; it was designed by the son of a local farmer as a thank-you for mentoring him. This logo was placed on everything from writing paper, sheets, carpets, and fabrics to notepads, umbrellas, biscuit tins, and aprons. He extrapolated the geometric H symbol into an entire alphabet, the letters of which became the wallpaper of my childhood.

From houses to gardens, restaurants to hotels, and jewelry to books, my father was a master of good taste. He taught many others how to make the world a lovelier place.

THE GROVE

In 1979, my father had been horrified to discover that they had to sell Britwell, although my mother was relieved. The idea of moving into a house that did not need an intimidating fleet of uniformed staff, including the chap who came once a week just to wind all the clocks and another whose sole job was to close up the endless shutters each night, was actually rather welcome. The Grove was nowhere near the scale of Britwell, but my father's brilliance still turned this small dower house into the perfect country home.

The Grove lies only a few fields away from Britwell, surrounded by more than half of the estate's land which my parents retained, so my mother's riding was uninterrupted, and my father set about creating a new home and extensive gardens. One of the first things he did was to cut through a wood at the far end of a view from the dining room. He always wanted the eye to travel, and this troublesome copse of trees did not allow for that. It was only after chain saws and tractors were sent in to cut the perfect keyhole through the woods that he realized he did not actually own it.

The stable block was finished first, of course, and the horses were moved into their new home while we still camped amid packing crates. Every morning as her horse was brought round, my mother would climb the mounting block with her hair chicly wrapped in a scarf, never a helmet. Whenever I was home from school, I would ride with her through the countryside, surprising the red kites (newly reintroduced birds of prey) who would spring up from the clearings in front of us, whistling in such a way that my mother always wondered if it was the noise of poachers.

My mother would return through the front door, which was guarded by two enormous-cast iron panthers that my father had given to her as a birthday present. She would remove her riding boots in the boot room, leaning against the bookcase built to hold my father's endless volumes of newspaper clippings and memorabilia. He always reminded us that if there were a fire, the first thing we were expected to save were these albums, and after those the family Bible and jewelry.

OPPOSITE: A George Romney painting—the one that made his career, in fact. This went away on tour a few years ago, and my father brought in a photographic copy with the same dimensions. Below the painting are Chinese vases that my father transformed into table lamps.

PAGES 52–53: Can you spot the two fake windows? My father had these painted onto the wall beside the porch. OPPOSITE AND ABOVE: The white-patterned china by Thomas Goode was on my mother's wedding registry fifty-five years ago. Fifty-five years seemed impressive till my mother reminded me that she had a piece of the Spanish Armada on her desk dating back to 1588.

Hampshire

PAGES 56–57: These scenes were originally painted by Rex Whistler in grisaille, turquoise, and silver for my grandmother, Edwina Mountbatten, in 1937, in the boudoir in her Park Lane apartment. Removed when the war started, the murals went to Broadlands for safekeeping. My father reassembled the panels for my mother twice, once at Britwell and then again in the dining room of the Grove. Out of sight is a depiction of my grandmother reclining naked with Father Time against the clock. (The butler was deeply shocked when he was shown this.) OPPOSITE: My father's maximalist swagging. ABOVE: Worlds collide: the preserved flower wreath I wore as a bridesmaid to the wedding of Prince Charles and Lady Diana sits among eighteenth-century ornamental Chinese white jade dishes.

A line of hooks on another wall held all the outdoor coats, hats, and bags, Burberry macs, Barbour coats, shooting jackets, cartridge bags, even a Stetson hat, given to my mother by Mr. Marcus of Neiman Marcus when she was in Texas to accompany my grandfather on an official visit. They were asked to bring tiaras for a black-tie evening; my mother traveled wearing her tiara hidden beneath a very fashionable velvet beret in order to avoid insurance issues.

Once changed from her boots and jodhpurs, my mother would resume her reading—as always—in the Regency drawing room my father had decorated.

In about 1805, when the Grove changed from a farmhouse to a dower house, the lack of a reasonable drawing room led a previous owner to add one for his widowed mother. When my parents moved in, there were still two windows on either side of the fireplace, which my father promptly had filled in, saying that the huge single window on the sidewall looking out onto the garden was plenty. There was also a population of squirrels who lived above the room and ate any wiring my father had installed.

My father had the walls of the drawing room covered with pale pink cotton. Amazingly, despite thirty-five years of log fires, they are still handsome. The ruffled swagged curtains (a trademark of my father's) have not been touched since they were first put up, mostly because we are afraid they would refuse to swag again. Indeed, my father's work is so timeless that the Grove has remained without significant alteration.

These days, my mother still likes to sit quietly in her pink drawing room reading, just as she did when my father was putting the finishing touches on their home. Being a marathon reader, her display of books spills over from the shelves and tables onto other available spaces. As a result, nobody has ever been able to sit on the stool by the fireplace.

My mother says she knew that there was absolutely no point getting involved in decorating the Grove, much to the perplexity of friends and visitors, who would ask her what the plans were. My mother says, "I never knew because I was reading. And really, what was the point of spoiling an expert's decoration with silly, ignorant suggestions?"

My father was never going to sit still, even after the house was completed, and no one, least of all my mother, would expect him to settle next to her on the drawing room sofa. In fact, I rarely remember him in this room, except for when guests would arrive for lunch or dinner, and they would have a drink in there together.

My father was very precise about time, and lunch was served at 1:15 p.m. on the dot. You were invited to arrive at 1:00 p.m., and God forbid if you arrived after the grandfather clock struck one in the hallway. I remember one poor couple showed up for lunch a day early, and my father sent them away, only to then discover that he had written the date down incorrectly. (I'm not sure if they ever came back.) He was also meticulous about plumping cushions.

OPPOSITE: A 1775 French clock, which chimes to this day, presides over the marble chimney breast. At first my mother told me that the bust was Louis XIV. She later called back a little sheepishly to say that it is, in fact, the Duke of Marlborough.

As children we knew that once the cushions were plumped, we were not to disturb such perfection, and thus we would head for the hard armchairs. I remember once the cushions had been plumped in advance of another decorator's arrival. My sister, in a wild moment, jumped feet first onto the sofa, de-plumping as she went. This was, of course, one of the bravest things I had ever witnessed: the de-plumping of David Hicks's cushions.

Throughout the house, there were "tablescapes" of various items. (My father claimed to have coined this term, which describes arrangements of objects in decorative groups, and who are we to question that?) These might range from a collection of blue lapis lazuli, enamel, pottery, or glass, to pink Indian rose quartz carved animals and snuffboxes.

My mother would try to add to these collections, and she learned early on that my father liked textured gold, so she gave him a ridged gold Cartier cigarette case as a wedding present, which turned out to be a bit of a disappointment, as he had been hoping for a Rolls-Royce. For his next birthday, my mother chose an antique lapis lazuli box with wavy edges—but he explained to her later that you can't have wavy edges with lapis lazuli. After that, my mother said, "Darling, you can buy your own birthday presents."

In the library, which was directly across the hall of waxed York flagstone from the drawing room, my father had created a warm, cozy room around my great-great-grandfather Sir Ernest Cassel's old desk, upon which stood his grandfather's gilt sphinx clock. Over the small chimney breast, my father stretched his grandmother's deep red velvet evening dress (upcycling way before anyone else). Scarlet leather–bound (and once the money ran out, red craft paper–bound) books crowded the shelves on either side of the fireplace. Other inherited leather-bound beauties lined the remaining walls. Even my father's oversize gardening albums found a home in an Egyptian-style freestanding mahogany bookcase on top of the Turkish rug.

My mother takes tea very seriously, and she normally enjoys it in the drawing room from a tray on her lap whilst seated under the seven portraits by George Romney beside the fire. If she is joined by guests, it is arranged in the dining room, in which my parents installed the panels by Rex Whistler that had hung first in my grandmother's boudoir and later in the drawing room of Britwell. The teapot was always heated first, and most afternoons you could spot my mother straining the tea into a saucer for her dachshund. "No one enjoys leaves in their tea," she would say.

After Whistler completed the grisaille, turquoise, and silver panels, my grandmother, Edwina Mountbatten, brought the butler in to show them off. He nodded approvingly as he looked around, until his eye caught sight of Father Time, lounging naked against the clock. And then he saw the depiction of my grandmother as Venus, also rather naked, sleeping on the other side. "Oh, no, my Ladyship," said the butler, "this will never do."

OPPOSITE: A collection of chinoiserie objects, some displayed on boxes my father covered by hand with Italian marbleized wrapping paper.

ABOVE: The handsome Empress Eugenie supervising the scene from my mother's side table, inside which she hides her Charbonnel et Walker rose and violet cream chocolates. OPPOSITE: The Paul de Lamerie inkwell on my mother's desk, untouched for quite some time, and the letter holder and blotter neatly hide paperwork that can't be faced.

CHRISTIES

Once my mother and I were sitting in the drawing room eating buttered crumpets when I asked her to remind me of the scenes Whistler had painted: all of the family homes; Sabi, her mother's pet lion cub; and classical motifs celebrating the sea, travel, gardening, and music. As she lifted one of the wood-handled teapots (one pot for Indian tea, one pot for China tea), she reminded me that the Fabergé bell she uses to summon someone from the kitchen was originally given to her grandmother, who left a note saying that when my mother reached her twenty-first birthday, she was to have the bell. Her grandmother was not only organized but also determined. At eighty-seven years old, she had simply decided that it was certainly time to die and she was not going to wake up the next morning, so you may imagine her frustration when she did. And she continued to do so for four more days, finally dying on the fifth day, but not before she had made use of the extra time by reminding her great friend Baroness Von Buxhoeveden to wear fleece-lined boots at her funeral because it was going to be cold that week.

Nearly as important to my mother as tea is breakfast, which happens in bed. Every morning a tray is brought into her apricot-colored bedroom, and a boiled egg and toast with local honey are eaten off the early twentieth century Hammersley china set, which my mother deems "very modern," and which must appear to be modern when you have a cabinet on the landing filled with china dating back to 1708.

On the wall above her tall chest of drawers hangs the famous portrait of my grandmother by Salvador Dalí. My grandmother had stepped into a Parisian elevator in the late 1930s to discover that her fellow passenger was the famous artist. As the lift brought them to their desired floor, Dalí became captivated by the tiny feet of this wealthy, glamorous, and much-photographed socialite; his gaze never left my grandmother's feet for the entire elevator ride.

PAGE 66: This antique snuffbox in the shape of a bullfinch would have been carried by a seventeenth-century lady in her "pocket," which was actually a small pouch. PAGE 67: Three Romney paintings and one Sir Henry Raeburn peacefully survey the drawing room. OPPOSITE: Looking out from the front door, my father's perambulating steeple could often be spotted in the far distance, confusing the uninitiated guest. My father could not resist the fun of designing an intricate porch—it was an excuse for more H logos in the far corners. Here is Domino, delighted at being left alone with the scissors, and the daffodils my father famously decided were the wrong shade of yellow and tried to remove from the wild grass in front of the house.

HUNTER

Dalí was fascinating to my grandmother, and he was fascinated by her. Essentially, my grandmother commissioned the portrait and paid for it, though Dalí approached her with the idea. I grew up with that picture, seeing it every day of my life in my mother's bedroom, and as a child I was also very frightened by it. Indeed, this work is highly characteristic of Dalí's style—my grandmother's curly hair becomes a Medusa-like nest of writhing snakes. Her lovely face, with its piercing blue eyes, has a deathly pallor, staring out at us from a landscape that appears primordial. My mother says that it's a very good likeness.

My father slept a little bit farther down the corridor in a room of modest proportions ("One likes one's own room in the autumn of one's life," he said) featuring two museum-like cabinets with delicate Gothic detailing holding gatherings of memorabilia: my grandfather's passport, a wind-up monkey band, Russian Easter eggs, a signed picture of Richard Nixon, letters from his mother. He slept on a half tester bed that matched the scale of the room, and his bath was in an alcove at the foot of the bed. If you happened to open what looked like a cupboard, you discovered it was, in fact, his loo. Around the washbasin were shelves of vellum books, and one little section revealed hinged false ones, where offensive things like a toothbrush and shaving cream were cunningly hidden.

My parents moved into the Grove in the winter of 1979. It had been an unbearably tragic year for my mother, as she had witnessed the assassination of her father by the IRA that summer. Having to sell Britwell the same year must have been profoundly sad in many ways, even if her new rural idyll offered an easier rhythm and spirit. And while the Grove may reflect some of the fancies and foibles of my flamboyant eccentric father, it remains to this day the home of my mother, an exquisite example of a well-lived life in the English countryside.

PAGE 70: My grandfather in naval uniform, painted by Philip de László. On the opposite side of the room hangs my grandmother's portrait as a young bride. PAGE 71: My great-great-grandfather, Sir Ernest Cassel, painted by the Swedish artist Anders Zorn, hangs in the Swedish room, above the fireguard embroidered by my grandfather's sister, the queen of Sweden. The frame has been cut in order to open a hidden doorway revealing the dressing room beyond. OPPOSITE: Underneath the Salvador Dalí portrait of my grandmother is a colored photograph of her wearing her coronation dress in 1937 and a Cartier cigarette case and matchbox (known as a chatelaine) that could be worn around your neck. A crystal peacock is from the former Czechoslovakia. PAGE 74: My mother has had breakfast in bed for as long as I can remember. Her routine is not to be messed with. PAGE 75: A display cabinet full of antique china is also not to be messed with. Those confusing black-painted bars under the shelves were another of my father's homemade touches. They ingeniously hid the harsh spotlights.

DECORATION
DEBORAH and PATRICK
DEVONSHIRE LEIGH FERMOR
THE MASTERWORKS
EGYPT

PAGES 76–77: My father's bedroom canopy is dressed in a chintz fabric that was saved from a bachelor guest room at Britwell. The white and cream vellum books belonged to my grandmother and came from her all-white boudoir. ABOVE AND OPPOSITE: My father created these cabinets to house curiosities from both his side of the family and my mother's.

MEMBERS OF THE
ASSISTANTS,
1876.
COPY OF FREEDOM
CITY OF LONDON
Bloc F
F14
ARWISGIAD TYWYSOG
NAVE SOUTH
DOME NORTH - A
Salters' Ha
ELECTION DAY,
MONDAY, JUNE 15th, 192
KINGHAM PALACE
7th June 1977
By Command of
AJESTY THE QUEEN
DHF
1973-1983
THE WHITE HOUSE
E DAVID HICKS SUIT

DAVID HICKS
VOL. 3 1961 1963
BRITWELL SALOME
DAVID HICKS
VOL. 4 1964 1965
BRITWELL SALOME
DAVID HICKS
VOL. 5 1965 1966
BRITWELL SALOME
DAVID HICKS
VOL. 6 1966 1968
BRITWELL SALOME
DAVID HICKS
VOL. 7 1968 1969
BRITWELL SALOME
DAVID HICKS
VOL. 8 1969 1970
BRITWELL SALOME
DAVID HICKS
VOL. 9 1970 1971
BRITWELL SALOME
DAVID HICKS
VOL. 10 1971 1972
BRITWELL SALOME
DAVID HICKS
VOL. 11 1973 1975
BRITWELL SALOME

DAVID HICKS
VOL. 13
1977 1978
BRITWELL SALOME
DAVID HICKS
VOL. 14
1979-1981
THE GROVE
DAVID HICKS
VOL. 15
1981-1982
THE GROVE
DAVID HICKS
VOL. 16
1982 1983
THE GROVE
DAVID HICKS
VOL. 17
1984-1986
THE GROVE
DAVID HICKS
VOL. 18
1986 1987
THE GROVE
DAVID HICKS
VOL. 19
1987 1988
THE GROVE
DAVID HICKS
VOL. 20
1988 1991
THE GROVE
DAVID HICKS
VOL. 21
1991 1992
THE GROVE

LOCK & Co
HATTERS,
St James's Street.
LONDON.

PAGES 80–81: My father always reminded us that if there were a fire, we should grab his series of scrapbooks first and the family Bible second. OPPOSITE: The boot room, with a wild assortment of hats including the Stetson given to my mother by Mr. Marcus of Neiman Marcus. ABOVE: A smorgasbord of vases. My father took flower arranging seriously.

IN HONOUR BOUND
FROM VICEREGAL LODGE SIMLA

OPPOSITE: My father said you should never knock on the door of a downstairs room, just open the door and walk in. Welcome to his library. ABOVE: More cleverness with Italian wrapping paper. Here, my father handcrafted a trial lampshade using it. PAGES 86–87: At great expense, my father re-covered a lot of the library books in red leather. At much less expense, he covered the breastplate above the fireplace with his mother's old velvet evening dress. PAGE 88: A young Queen Victoria stands out against the velvet breastplate. PAGE 89: I grew up playing card games like racing demon and canasta. Twiglets were always on offer. You can see those funny wheat-and-Marmite snacks in the Halcyon Days tray my father designed for them.

MAHARAJAS' JEWELS
INDIAN SUMMER
HOLY BIBLE

BURKE'S
PEERAGE
Sir William Chambers
WHISTLER
INDIA
A LONELY BUSINESS

VIEWS & VISTAS

Not once would I dare to complain about my tropical existence, but every so often during the winter months a tiny emotion stirs deep inside, reminding me that I grew up in gardens of frost, not fronds.

When my parents moved into Britwell the grounds were already very established, but at the Grove my father dedicated himself to the grounds' design for the last nineteen years of his life. It was here that he applied the principles of interior design to the outdoors, pushing back the boundaries of gardening on a grand scale.

It's fascinating that his passion for design developed to focus on the garden, but then he always said that gardens are organic spaces, maturing and ripening once you have laid them out. They are much more interesting than rooms, which usually do not age quite as well. And by this time in his life, my father was perhaps beginning to realize that he wasn't immortal and that what he was creating in Oxfordshire would easily outlive him.

He alternated his interior-design commissions with the relief of coming home to plant and refine, develop, rip out, and replace until he had the garden at the Grove just as he wanted. It is a garden full of surprises and complexity, with doors in walls that open onto secret spaces, a bridge over a moat, pyramid-topped gateposts, allées of stilted hornbeam trees with hornbeam hedges beneath them, and broad sweeps of manicured lawn, turning the old farmhouse garden into a dazzling display of imagination—a garden that many travel far and wide to see to this day.

As always, he took his influences from the early eighteenth century, more particularly from Anglo-French traditions. For my father, gardening became an extension of his meticulously controlled design techniques. The garden itself—in terms of the views and the "rooms"—became an extension of the house.

OPPOSITE: A Grove vista in summer sunshine. PAGE 92: Winter whites. PAGE 93: Naked autumn.

He loved avenues and vistas; he always professed to being "very much a straight-line gardener." He always began with the view from a principal room in the house, the dining room, the drawing room, an upstairs bedroom. "For much of the year, one's main enjoyment will be from the inside," he said, "so the first thing is to get the main vista sorted. Then you can embroider in between."

Nevertheless, his embroidery remained quite monochrome; the local ladies were mystified. Where were all the flowers? It wasn't that he disliked flowers, it was just that he preferred not to see them growing.

Good long lines lead the eye everywhere at the Grove. The long-suffering gardeners were "advised" to mow very, very straight, neat lines to improve the lines of sight. And my father —with great pride—had the long vista from the dining room window "improved," Capability Brown-style, by cutting down several trees from an irritating avenue a couple of miles across the fields that blocked the "eye."

The tree-lined allées (of pleached chestnut and paneled hornbeam) and vistas at the Grove run from three of the sides of the house to create and enclose a sequence of ten "rooms." Rooms which are either, for the most part, deeply—greenly—formal, or lush in their abundance. The rose garden my father planted falls into the latter category. If I close my eyes, I can capture the smell of warm English rain, freshly mown grass, and rose and peony petals. I created a fragrance inspired by this rose garden.

Like so many other aspects of my father's scheme, the rose garden is both secret and a surprise—with its Lutyens seat, it becomes a lovely sitting room where, in summer, you cannot be seen at all. My father was far too busy to ever sit there. He did plan, however, that it would be the place in which my sister and I were proposed to—a heaven-scented backdrop to one of life's dramatic moments—unless, of course, we were proposed to by one of the dukes on the list he kept in his desk drawer. If the proposal came from a duke, then it would obviously happen on his grand ducal estate. Each time one of the dreaded dukes married someone else, he was scratched off my father's list. No proposals of the sort ever happened, but it wasn't for want of him designing it.

The test of a good garden, he would say, is seeing it in winter, which is exactly when Rosemary Verey, the doyenne of English garden design, interviewed him on camera about his choices and design. The snow lay crisp and even that day, and my father was pleased that the venerable Ms. Verey drew the viewers' attention to the fact that the effect of the "wonderful shadows cast by the strong winter sun" was "quite architectural." "Structure is everything," my father replied, as he stalked about dressed in his favorite cloak.

PAGE 94: Moments around the Grove garden, including sightings of my father's Pavilion, a birthday present to himself. PAGE 95: The naked discus thrower (bottom right) can always embarrass guests, but they are enchanted by my grandmother's profile surrounded by Bahamian coral and shells (bottom left). OPPOSITE: The goddess Flora keeping cool in the shade of my mother's garden.

There is careful attention to detail everywhere. He used statues and urns for symmetry, and everything is in perfect proportion. The sentry-like containers create focal points without adding color. (Container gardening was actually a brilliant cheat—all of the plants look as if they are planted in containers, but in fact they are planted in the soil below, negating the need for watering.)

My father also loved texture: "Different materials have different textures you can play with, such as brick, stone, pebbles, clapboard, and even water," he once told a journalist. "The leaves of certain plants have fantastically interesting textures—hostas have those fabulous grooves, bergenias are leathery, artichokes have that silvery spikiness. Then if you want to add flowers you can, but the garden does not collapse without them."

Never one for wavering indecision, he had long decided that bright blue pools were vulgar, so when ours was built, it was painted black. The unsuspecting daffodils were the wrong shade of yellow, so he ran them over furiously in his Range Rover as best he could—and they always grew back, perhaps a little stronger for the attention.

The garden may be an extension of the house, but it also extends further afield. One of his favorite inventions was a perambulating spire; from across the fields, it looked like one of the grand English country-house monuments or follies. It actually had an ingenious three-sided design and was variously a pyramid or a church spire or an obelisk depending on which side he cared to display at that distance. Ever practical and always designing with an engineer's bent, he made it out of plywood and strapped it to an old shepherd's cart so it could be moved about the landscape to provide a focus at the end of a vista or obliterate the view of village roofs. Visiting guests often thought they were losing their minds, as it appeared as if the church spire had moved from one day to the next.

For his sixtieth birthday, my father gave himself a moated and turreted Gothic garden pavilion overlooking the secret rose garden. It was built to his exacting vision, situated in a corner of the garden between green avenues and vistas, and surrounded by a small moat, across which lay a little wooden bridge that could be wound up by a mechanical pulley.

One day, while showing a group of Japanese visitors around the garden, my father strode across the bridge, leaving the visitors on the other side to watch as he theatrically showed off his pulley system to wind up the bridge. Unfortunately, the pulley failed about halfway, and the bridge became stuck upright. The Japanese stood politely on one side of the moat wondering if this was part of the show, and my father stood on the other side wondering how the hell he was going to get back across the water.

PAGE 98: The rose garden where my father imagined I might romantically get engaged. I must have caused such disappointment. PAGE 99: A soggy afternoon, but the smell of those wild roses makes up for it. PAGE 101: Moonlight over the clipped hornbeam hedges.

It was in this pavilion that my father's open coffin was laid for the few days leading up to his funeral, so his family could say a proper farewell and he could lie in the peace and quiet of his garden. His own funeral was the final thing my father designed. Everything was arranged entirely according to his directions, which he had written down in a small notebook. The coffin, without handles (those were far too common), was made from gray-stained sycamore as he directed and lined with one of his own fabrics. After the viewing, it was carried by his gardeners and my brother across the little moat of his pavilion and laid on an ivy-covered trailer behind his Range Rover, as he was driven away for the last time from the garden he had so lovingly created.

PAGES 102–103: A perfect example of my father's precise planning for a symmetrical garden. PAGES 104–105: Evening falling over the Pavilion, also known fondly as Grump Tower. OPPOSITE: The inspiration behind my English Rose fragrance, to which I added the scents of warm rain and mown grass.

PAGES 108–109: England in surprising sunshine. OPPOSITE: The wooden planters you see here were designed not to have a bottom, encouraging the plants in them to feed from the soil directly in the ground and be self-sustaining. ABOVE: Bathed in evening light, the little drawbridge can be seen over the moat around the Pavilion.

PART 2

THE NEW TRADITION

AMERICA FARM

"You cannot begin to build until the birds and bees have stopped breeding," said the representative from the South Oxfordshire District Council. What? David and I were confused. "And then there has to be the bat survey. If bats are living in the area, you won't be able to do anything. . . ." Part of me was thrilled that someone was looking out for the birds, the bees, and the bats. But another part of me was terrified—if there was a bat about, we could not build our new home.

A few years prior, David and I had decided to build on a small parcel of land I owned close to my mother. All we wanted to do was to build a home very much in keeping with the local architecture, a home that would look really old and not new at all. However, the complications were many: Apart from the birds, the bees, and the bats, there was the fact that our builder had movie-star looks, which meant I had to get extra dressed-up every time we went for a meeting. And we needed a license to remove the asbestos from the two existing 1970s structures on the property. (I thought asbestos was evil, why did we need a license to remove it?) In addition, the South Oxfordshire District Council were giving us a really hard time with our proposed plans.

After several months of back and forth, our plans were approved. We had adjusted the pitch of the roof, we had twisted the house by a few apparently crucial inches, and we had battled over roof slates. Spanish slates are less expensive than Welsh ones, but were they prettier? It was hard to spend unnecessary money on slates—you don't often get the chance to show them off. ("Oh, do come over and look at our new slates.") In the end, we went with the Spanish ones at a considerable savings. David said, "You had us at 'hola!'"

By now David, accustomed to the warmer climes of the tropics, had discovered that the nearby village of Benson and its surroundings are known to be southern Britain's coldest spot. He immediately added another fireplace to our design.

The biggest argument that we had during the two years it took to build America Farm was over one small bathroom door handle. We simply could not agree and silently sulked for days over this. In the end, this small battle receded in the excitement at finishing our new house.

PAGE 112: A fraction of what goes on in the garden at America Farm when Conrad is home from school. OPPOSITE: We are slaves to symmetry. Even David's 1964 Alfa Romeo has to be perfectly centered on the door to America Farm when parked.

UPSTAIRS

Once we had planning permission it was full tilt ahead, although designing and decorating a home long-distance whilst simultaneously building a new company certainly tested our organizational skills, patience, bank account, and belief in the project. But just as my company laid its foundations, so did America Farm, named for the field it rests upon.

I think having lived so long in the tropics with bare floorboards and cool tiles, we could not face traditional carpeting upstairs and instead felt wall-to-wall sisal was the way to go. The only problem is, What happens when someone spills hot chocolate? Does the entire carpet have to be ripped out, or just the arms of the culprit?

Luckily, the builders we worked with also had an impressive joinery setup, so all of our windows were made to fit. They even gave Wesley, our eldest son and a carpentry enthusiast, an internship. Wesley was instrumental in making the two circular windows that sit centrally on the facade of the house.

These builders also crafted our four-poster bed, which we covered in a quiet Chinese toile from Bennison; painted the room the palest of blues; and slipped in a Meridienne fireplace sofa (which has one arm lower to take the heat from a fire) that appeared to have been measured to perfection.

Because the house was newly built, we had the luxury of adding radiant heating beneath the marble floor in our bathroom and the flagstones in the kitchen, making them more welcoming to our sensitive Bahamian feet. David lined the bathroom shelves with Penguin paperbacks and cleverly filled the cut-glass decanters he had inherited from his father with brightly colored bubble bath. We hung three Matisse nudes above the towel rail as a finishing touch.

OPPOSITE: Bedside-table books yield old photos—memories acting as bookmarks. PAGE 118: Between our bedroom windows sits a French Empire méridienne (a fireside sofa to you and me), a vintage Stella McCartney military jacket, and a Danish interior painting by Niels Holsøe. PAGE 119: The four-poster bed is dressed with a Chinese toile fabric by Bennison, the portrait is of Beatrice Cenci after one by Guido Reni, and the roses are from the garden. I could sleep for a thousand years in this room if there was ever time.

FULL TILT
Ireland to India
with a Bicycle
LOL!
ILove
Photobooths .co.uk

GOOD DOG
GARDEN GUN
The Last Love Song
TRACY DAUGHERTY
THE FLYING CLASSROOM
ERICH KASTNER
EMIL AND THE THREE TWINS
ERICH KASTNER

OPPOSITE: A French Empire mahogany secretaire in my bedroom, for those times when my study downstairs is hijacked by the children and I still have late-night meetings with the office in California. ABOVE: A small white treasure chest designed by me with a gold token on the front engraved with the words "Live an extraordinary life."

OPPOSITE: Domino chilling on top of Wesley, one of her four long-suffering brothers. ABOVE: Truly the height of luxury: a dressing room with simple ticking fabric lining the cupboards, anchored by my mother's vast Fortnum & Mason hatbox.

Burlington

As the house neared completion and the scaffolding came down, we began to think in earnest about who would sleep where. We realized that the room designated the linen cupboard could potentially be the prettiest bedroom of all and was in danger of being utterly wasted, so we hunted for any other spare cupboard or space that we could relocate the linens to and transformed this room into a single guest room. We decorated it with walls of black-and-white ticking fabric, inspired by a room we had seen by the brilliant decorator Veere Grenney. Thick ticking-stripe curtains could close off the single bed, and a bright yellow blanket from Nicaragua, the color of rapeseed, was used as a bedspread like a exclamation mark.

We had the carpenter custom make a cupboard to fit the tiny dimensions of this room and finished it with antiqued mirror glass to make it feel foxed. Inside, I hung the silver and gold–thread garlands that had been presented to my mother when she was visiting the Maharaja of Jaipur—a hidden surprise for anyone staying long enough to unpack.

Across the hall is Felix's room. As he is now out of school and living in the house more than anyone else, he chose to have contrasting Coca-Cola red and gunmetal gray stripes painted diagonally from one corner to another. The campaign bed frame was my father's from Albany in London. I had it re-covered in my Heritage geometric fabric.

Felix's youngest brother, Conrad, wanted to sleep in bunk beds, which I thought was a fab idea; David felt otherwise. It would ruin the look of a perfectly proportioned room, he said. Conrad got his bunk beds, but to ameliorate David's anguish, we had them built to feel as nautical as possible. Flush-mounted ring pulls were used on the drawers, and simple linen curtains on brass rods close off each of the four bunks. The walls were painted navy blue, and my grandfather's standard hung between the windows. It last flew over Classiebawn Castle in Ireland before being taken down after his death. Conrad wanted the walls to be painted orange, which made even me nervous, so we compromised with an armchair upholstered in a deep orange velvet and a matching cushion framed in an Ashley Hicks fabric sample.

Domino's bedroom was at the far end of the corridor, painted in the faintest of pinks. It's a sunny, bright room, with three windows overlooking the barns across the lane. She sleeps in my mother's bed, also inherited from the Albany, which is dressed in an original David Hicks patterned fabric with a very David Hicks pelmet.

In acrylic boxes on the far wall hang two dresses, one the dress my mother wore as a bridesmaid to the Queen, the other I wore as a bridesmaid to Prince Charles and Princess Diana.

PAGE 124: Domino prepares to dive into our bathtub, the mirrored shelves lined with cut-glass decanters full of bubble bath and Penguin Classics paperbacks. PAGE 125: Matisse nudes in my bathroom, lithographs in very good old frames. OPPOSITE: This was originally intended to be the linen room—but given its view over the fields and its size, it seemed a waste of the space—so we plagiarized the work of the great designer Veere Grenney. Imitation is the sincerest form of flattery.

SUSPENSE
ARDUUS
SOLEM

PAGES 128–129: Felix's bedroom, the walls decorated in gunmetal and red, a color scheme inspired by his father's E-Type Jaguar. The paintings are by Felix, and I'm almost happy to trade off the fear of oil paint on sisal carpets for seeing him produce these. OPPOSITE: Hanging in Conrad's bedroom is the standard (the flag) of my grandfather, which was flying from his home at Classiebawn when he was assassinated in 1979. ABOVE: Conrad's bedroom has built-in bunk beds for an overflow of friends and cousins. David campaigned strongly against the bunk bed proposal. We made them as nautical as possible in order to seduce him into the idea.

My mother had been in India leading up to the wedding of the Queen and Prince Philip—my grandfather was trying to hand back power—so she had missed most of her dress fittings. Her dress features a tight waist, a full skirt, and layers of tulle over white netting petticoats, which are sprinkled with star-shaped lily heads created from seed pearls and crystal beads. The dress is set off perfectly by a delicate tiara of silver orange blossoms and ears of corn.

OPPOSITE AND ABOVE: Domino sleeps in a bed inherited from her grandmother tented in her grandfather's fabric, originally in a room with matching fabric on the walls, chairs, dressing table, bedspread and even coat hangers. My father enjoyed statements. The delightful little green velvet cape my mother wore to the King's coronation. PAGES 134–135: Scrapbook pages commemorating my and my mother's turns as royal bridesmaids. And wow, my haircut stank (top right).

of the Household
by Her Majesty to invite
and Lady Pamela Hicks
Buckingham Palace
The Queen and The Duke of Edinburgh
27th July, 1981
of His Royal Highness
Lady Diana Spencer
White Tie
or
Black Tie

Layout of the
State Apartments
for the
RECEPTION
at
Buckingham Palace
on
Row B
HIS ROYAL HIGHNESS
Chamberlain
Dean
Please see over
and, right, India Hicks
Clementine Hambro enjoying

Hanging next to my mother's bridesmaid dress is mine. When my godfather, the Prince of Wales, called to ask if I would like to be a bridesmaid, I was initially horrified. I was a 13-year-old tomboy never out of jodhpurs, but I would have to wear a dress. Charles was a remarkable godfather,—caring, considerate, and involved—and I adored him and still do. So despite my reservations about the dress, I glowed with pride at having been asked.

I met Diana for the first time at one of her dress fittings at the lily-strewn studio of designers David and Elizabeth Emanuel. When we arrived, Diana was upstairs on the special floor where her dress was kept under lock and key. The windows of the entire building had been blocked out so that the press camped on rooftops across the street could not snap a shot of the dress, as it was one of the most closely guarded fashion secrets in history.

On the eve of the wedding, we joined members of the royal family, visiting dignitaries, and glamorous film stars—including Princess Grace of Monaco—for the firework display in Hyde Park. The London sky lit up as fireworks exploded in time to Handel's *Music for the Royal Fireworks*, ending with a spectacular revolving sun 170 feet above ground, which shot out sparkling flares.

Hundreds of thousands of people had gathered in the city for what turned out to be an incredible party. But anyone who has experienced a street party like this knows that getting home afterward is not so easy. The Queen was able to nip back to Buckingham Palace, but everyone else was pretty much stuck. Princess Margaret, mother of Sarah Armstrong-Jones, the chief bridesmaid, sensed my mother's concern about getting me to bed at a decent hour, so she offered to take me back to her apartment at Kensington Place for the night.

The following morning, Sarah and I rode in a sleek Daimler to Clarence House, home of the Queen Mother, where Diana had spent the night. Scarlet-coated footmen showed us upstairs to a nursery floor, where Diana was having her hair done, dressed in jeans and a T-shirt. Beside her on a small dressing table was a tiny television set with a rather grainy reception so she could watch the wedding preparations going on across London, which were interspersed with images and stories of her past. She got very cross if someone stood in the way.

Just after 10:00 a.m., Diana stepped out of her jeans and into her fairy-tale ivory silk taffeta wedding gown with its dramatic twenty-five-foot train. While she, accompanied by her father, Earl Spencer, slowly made her way to St. Paul's, Sarah and I were standing by in the chapel of St. Michael and St. George, one of the many smaller chapels inside the cathedral.

It took Diana—on the shaky arm of her father, with five bridesmaids and two pages in attendance—three and a half minutes to walk up the aisle in front of the biggest gathering of European and foreign royals ever, an invited congregation of 3,500, plus that vast television audience. Can you imagine having 3,000 people at your wedding?

The Archbishop of Canterbury led the traditional Church of England service, assisted by clergymen from many denominations. The bride's nerves showed briefly when she mixed up Charles's names, calling him Philip Charles, rather than Charles Philip. Inside that calm cathedral one could hear a pin drop, but outside on the steps and in the streets the nation roared in jubilation. I only really remember my buttercup-yellow satin shoes pinching, though, as they were a size too small.

After the private signing of the register, the Prince and Princess of Wales walked back down the aisle to Elgar's Pomp and Circumstance. Then I rode back to Buckingham Palace in a glass coach drawn by horses, an experience only slightly ruined by the tiny tears of fellow bridesmaid six-year-old Catherine Cameron, who turned out to be desperately allergic to horses and spent most of the journey miserably blowing her little nose on her petticoats.

My mother, who was a lady-in-waiting to Queen Elizabeth, had spent much of her life waving to crowds and gave me firm instructions: "You must wave," she warned me. "People don't want to see you ride past without waving." I did my best timid little waves to the joyous crowds.

The newlyweds took an open-topped carriage to Buckingham Palace, where they emerged on the balcony to give the crowds the kiss they had been longing to see. I had been privileged enough to have been on that famous balcony several times before, but nothing could have prepared me for the sight of the crowds that day.

Finally, the wedding breakfast. God knows why it's referred to as such because, in fact, it is a lunch. Brill in lobster sauce, and chicken stuffed with lamb mousse was served. I ate the bread rolls. Strawberries and cream followed.

Being royal, Charles had not one, but two best men. Princes Andrew and Edward made speeches, light and witty, just as you would imagine brothers would at a wedding. Then as soon as the cake had been cut, Diana, her sisters, and the bridesmaids disappeared upstairs to help her change into her going-away outfit.

And then they were gone, to begin their honeymoon at my grandfather's home, Broadlands. The married couple was whisked away across the Buckingham Palace courtyard with a wobbly "Just Married" sign and old Coke cans attached to the carriage by Prince Andrew and Prince Edward—raising smiles from the Queen, the Queen Mother, and Princess Margaret, who hotfooted it after them. It's not often you see the sovereign, her mother, and her sister all running across the palace courtyard.

My mother's royal bridesmaid dress and mine have been on display in museums and on tours around the world, but now they rest side by side, happy to have been part of history, but just as happy to be quietly hanging in America Farm.

& CO. (LONDON)
THOMAS GOODE & CO
(LONDON) LTD.

DOWNSTAIRS

Here, in David's words, is the journey of America Farm:

Although India and I had lived in the West Indies for more than twenty years, the time finally came to have a home in our native England. Our children had grown up barefoot, chasing snakes up coconut trees and playing pirate with machetes, so we decided to civilize them with British sports and Anglocentric history. What British mother's heart does not soar when her son can recite the batting order—"divorced, beheaded, died, divorced, beheaded, survived"—of Henry VIII's wives?

For a decade we crisscrossed the Atlantic, trying to make sure that hardly a weekend went by without the boys seeing at least one of us. During this time we had been guests in Oxfordshire of India's mother, Lady Pamela Hicks, widow of David, the celebrated decorator. But even she—survivor of the Blitz, the Partition of India, and acts of terrorism—could not be expected to endure Romneys and Raeburns swept off walls by indoor rugby matches, or tea trays shattered by cricket balls knocked through windows by malodorous, rampaging teenagers.

India was lucky enough to have some farmland near (but not too near) her mother, at the edge of the village where our boys had been christened. We had permission from the authorities to take down two 1970s farmworkers' cottages and build our idea of a house, with a small garden alongside large fields.

OPPOSITE: Now finally having a house of our own, I was able to unpack, appreciate, and above all use this set of china, which had been stored in the depths of my mother's basement since it was given to me, piece by piece, over birthdays and Christmases, by a clever, beloved godfather during my childhood. I was never going to risk shipping it to the Bahamas.

OPPOSITE: Cane-handled horsehair fly switches on the hall table. ABOVE: A French Deco sofa sits beneath an almost Japanese-style painting of the mountains at Rougemont by our son, Felix, as a schoolboy.

EUROPEAN UNION
UNITED KINGDOM OF GREAT BRITAIN AND NORTHERN IRELAND
PASSPORT
DENNIS
the
MENACE
FAN
YOU'LL SORT THAT BULLY OUT, WON'T YOU, ROGER?

PAGES 142–143: In the hall stand my grandmother's riding boots; outside stands David's preferred version of horsepower: a 1966 Mercedes Cabriolet. OPPOSITE: A telephone covered in decoupage cartoon pages from the children's comic *The Dandy* that we all grew up reading. ABOVE: An alcove with a Regency-style desk facing onto the fields, sporting candlestick lamps designed by my father in the 1970s but bought recently at auction.

OPPOSITE AND ABOVE: French Empire commodes flank the Portland stone fireplace we designed with Jamb. On one sits a generous bar setup and on the other, plaster objects from the British Museum along with prints and drawings that David is too indecisive to hang. The cross-legged ottoman was a housewarming gift from my brother, Ashley, who designs and makes them.

SCHATZBERG WOMEN THEN
Codex Seraphinianus
THE SWEDISH COUNTRY HOUSE
TIEPOLO
IN ANOTHER LIGHT

"If we are going to make this work," India said to me at that stage, "there is going to have to be a lot of compromise." The cold hand of fear gripped my heart as I had a flashback to a meeting twenty-five years earlier in my past life as an advertising man. A rather fierce client had asked me during a stressful creative pitch, "David, do you know what compromise means?" I replied, "Yes, meeting in the middle." With the look of one of those animals that eat their children, she coldly countered, "No, it means doing things you don't want to do." Months after that, I left England and that particular career.

"So what is your idea of a house in the country?" Andrew Nichols, our architect, asked. Here we got lucky: India and I both wanted something traditional, probably white stucco, a cross between a Danish farmhouse and a Georgian rectory. As a shorthand description I said, "We'd like to live in a Merchant Ivory film like everybody else, I suppose."

We are also complete slaves to symmetry in architecture. Aligning doors and windows is important as they create vistas that expand space. And living in the tropics had taught us that the breezes that pass through opposing windows and French doors would come in handy during England's two weeks of summer.

For the more predictable weather conditions, I was keen to have as many fireplaces as possible through the house. Whilst India loves nothing more than walking in biblical conditions of rain, sleet, and snow, I prefer to gaze upon inclement weather, sitting in the vicinity of crackling logs with a good book and a drink, so we had a Portland stone mantel made for the sitting room and a marble one for the study. I was very keen for another real fire in our bedroom, but India felt that clearing out an upstairs hearth would be a bore. Gingerly, I pointed out that it would be unusual for her to clean any hearth—we compromised with an artificial fire.

Though India grew up with vibrating palettes in every room, we tended to go with fairly neutral backgrounds and one keynote color, such as the orange Ultrasuede on my Louis XVI–style chairs. One of our sons' rooms has gunmetal-and-red-striped walls painted on the diagonal; our daughter's has a lit à la polonaise, covered in David Hicks's original Tumbling Rose print that was inherited from the Hicks family's famous Albany set. Art often supplies the chance to add color, with Gerald Laing's *Baby Baby Wild Things* and Alexander Calder lithographs being good cases in point. My antique gouaches of Vesuvius erupting and the eighteenth-century still-lifes, though, tend to find themselves "compromised" and lean against walls.

In the mixing of furniture that either I had collected or that India's parents had at Albany, we could not have been luckier—it all went together. The first night the seven of us stayed in the house, it felt like home.

OPPOSITE: An English "drum" or "rent" table is surrounded by my mother's rather amazing Napoleonic bergères covered in fabric by my father. Fascinatingly, the insurance appraiser knew from records that one is original eighteenth-century and the rest are copies, but the copies are so good that he couldn't distinguish which was which.

PAGE 150: A close-up of the arms of the Napoleonic chairs—swans were the symbol of the Empress Josephine. PAGE 151: A Georgian mirror and console, inherited from my parents, along with vellum scroll boxes, which acted like a rather large envelope at a grand ceremony. These belonged to my ancestor, Lord Palmerston. We lighten them up by putting my mother's swimming caps on display—almost like Pop Art topiary. OPPOSITE: In my study is a large oil painting that Felix did for his father. I adore this, so I've stolen it. ABOVE: Thistles, thyme, lavender and wild roses. The madness of home-grown, home-arranged flowers in jam jars and mustard pots.

PAGES 154–155: My study shows that I am my father's daughter. It contains orange Ultrasuede-covered antique French chairs and an equally orange print from the Gerald Laing 1968 Pop Art series *Baby Baby Wild Things*. Interestingly, the sisal rug you can barely see on the floor is real and has to be dampened every so often. ABOVE: Standing in the garden with lovely cow parsley from the hedgerows and some rather alarming finds from a local garden center—inexplicable but jolly. OPPOSITE: The kitchen has a huge table of reclaimed oak and iron along with Hans Wegner Wishbone chairs. The floor is warm tumbled limestone flagstone.

PAGE 158: Countryside goodness: apples from the garden, and blueberries and beetroot, from, well the supermarket. PAGE 159: Our Belgium bluestone countertop is well populated under the pendant lamps and beside the inexpensive industrial stools. ABOVE: A movie poster from the 1970s, a pastiche of James Bond aimed at the men in my life. OPPOSITE: Felix at work in the barn, which he seems to have claimed as a studio.

Albany
Dulux TRADE
Macpherson
TRADE PAINTS
ACRYLIC PRIMER UNDERCOAT
WHITE
Dulux TRADE
VINYL MATT
Nitro

PAGE 162: Flowers stolen from my parents' rose garden. PAGE 163: The garden room, or mudroom, miraculously clean and orderly. My sister Edwina's pale green fabric is the hero. ABOVE AND OPPOSITE: If ever we feel homesick for the tropics, we stand in this bathroom and breathe in the view of the palm fronds. The bookstand trolley was from Kensington Place and has KP carved on the underside to prove it. My mother's grandmother (the granddaughter of Queen Victoria) had apartments there when she was widowed. Spot the photograph of Prince Charles at his Investiture, aged twenty; this is when he became the Prince of Wales.

OPPOSITE AND ABOVE: I upholstered the walls of our guest room in a wool fabric, called Stirling Square Steel, created by Ronda Carman, a blogger and designer I admire. It perfectly matched the masculinity of the art and furniture, a vast mahogany Empire daybed and a painting in the style of Veronese depicting the Romans being beastly to St. Agatha.

AMERICA FARM
EWELME
WALLINGFORD
AMERICA FARM
EWELME
WALLINGFORD
FOR TOP BANANA —
REMEMBER TO BUY
TUCK FOR THE BOYS
TO TAKE BACK TO
SCHOOL -
AND CONRAD'S RUGBY
BOOTS FOR HIS
MATCH ON SATURDAY -
IS DOMINO HAVING
RIDING LESSON
PLUS
FOR TEA
CORINTHIA

who ran for a
City worker Jamie
Ramsay ran solo for

PAGE 168: There is something quite grown-up about really good stationery, especially when accessorized with tissue-lined envelopes. PAGE 169: I get very Virgo with the kindling and newspapers that start our fires. ABOVE AND OPPOSITE: Cars. Old cars. With a family of seven, David attempts to prove that a 1966 Mercedes Cabriolet is a practical mode of transport. Compared to the E-Type Jaguar with only two seats, it is.

ABOVE: Old wood and new wood: A 1820s chest of drawers waits in the woodshed to be found a home. OPPOSITE: The loft above the garage and woodshed is decorated like a bachelor's studio. It was seized by Amory, whose romantic tastes it seemed to answer, before the paint was even dry. PAGES 174–175: Amory's world, with Alexander Calder lithographs, a sleigh bed, a zebra-skin rug, and scaffolding planks for flooring. PAGES 176–177: Sitting in a window at America Farm and counting my blessings, which are many.

SAGE

ARMITE
EXTRACT

MARMITE & MINCE PIES

There are many traditions that ground our life here in England. Two things that are particularly English are big breakfasts and making things work, like china you don't think suits you yet somehow becomes a part of life, occasionally joined by sterling silver teaspoons with a royal crest.

"Oh, that was years ago," said my daughter Domino, aged eight. "I was seven when that happened." We were looking at photographs over breakfast on a cool October morning, and I realized the passing of time in Domino's mind was something quite different than in my mind.

I had set the breakfast table the evening before for guests who were staying for a few days. Although we often ate breakfast on the vintage English Adams china set, we did not normally put out the hand-embroidered napkins, both the teapot and coffee pot, choices of fresh orange or green juice, and the sterling silver teaspoons engraved with the Prince of Wales's coat of arms.

This was just over-the-top stuff to impress our guests, who were actually much more mesmerized by the fact that my son Conrad could eat not only two eggs and lashings of bacon, but also a stack of pancakes swimming in syrup as well as a mountain of toast and Marmite. English boarding schools will do that to you. You ate gigantic breakfasts because the rest of the meals were truly crap. The other thing you did was lick your cutlery as you sat down. Well, in my day you did. We would rush into the dining room, find an empty seat, grab the cutlery laid out, and lick it to mark our spot. Would you sit down somewhere if you were at risk of pre-licked cutlery? No, I didn't think so. It's a very effective way of saving your spot when you did get up to get your Frosties.

We inherited this pink-and-red English scenic china from my partner David's mother. It was all in perfect order, not a chip or crack in sight. At first I was a little unsure, as it was a color and pattern I would not normally have chosen, but now these dishes are part of the fabric of our family life in the countryside. I tried to explain to Domino how long ago I had first eaten breakfast off the plates—when David took me to meet his parents—but I realized her mind might explode at the thought of all those years.

PAGE 178: A silver water jug recommissioned as a vase. Marmite and toast, an English staple, is served at any time of the day or night. ABOVE AND OPPOSITE: We set up dinner in our barn for special occasions, which involves hanging a big old oil painting on the beam, lighting endless candles, and scattering wild English roses down the tables.

WALKERS
WALKERS

I sometimes say there's a bit of gypsy in me, and maybe that's why each summer we make sure not to miss Giffords Circus, a rollicking miniature-village-green circus started by an Oxford graduate who grew up putting on her own backyard circus with her sister using a borrowed tent from the local church that they adorned with cutout cardboard stars and flowers. It's an old-fashioned show, one that is uniquely English, with a caravan of jugglers, cockerels, lovers, horsemen and horsewomen, dreamers, acrobats, and musical ponies, staged under colored tents and sparkling lights.

PAGE 182: My mother came for tea, and she nearly fainted when she saw Domino had the fairy cakes on the 1708 Meissen plates. PAGE 183: My mother was much happier when her treacle tart sat on a more modern plate. OPPOSITE AND ABOVE: If Domino could, she would run off and join the circus.

At home we keep things simple, but sometimes one wants to put up a tent even when ballerinas on horseback aren't involved. Five days before a recent birthday, David asked how I wanted to celebrate it. "I don't," I said grumpily. Forty-nine is such a boring number. Four days before my birthday, I woke up thinking that that was exactly the reason to celebrate it.

Three days before my birthday, I hired a small tent called, exotically, a Chinese hat. "Why is there a marquee in the garden?" David asked.

My birthday fell on the American holiday of Labor Day, which meant our offices were closed, so I spent the day getting all Martha Stewart-y (except for the cooking bit, which I'm useless at). Down the middle of the tables, we laid long arms of wild blackberries picked in the lane, dried poppy heads from the fields, and fresh flowers grown in the garden, not because we thought they looked rather fab, but because we discovered we didn't have any vases.

And then I sewed, yes sewed, the blackberry and acorn branches onto the ends of the burlap runner. "Errr, what are you doing, Mum?" asked Conrad, while looking at me oddly. That morning, he had written me a card: *Hope you have an amazing PERTY.* And I did. With close friends and family beside me, I had an amazing perty.

To me family is everything, and we do all we can to overcome logistical challenges so as many of us as possible can be together for special days. Upon occasion, this seems to involve a bit of multigenerational time travel.

My mother no longer wants to take the journey of two flights, three cars, one golf cart, and a boat in order to spend Christmas with me in the Bahamas. She says her old knees object. This makes me very sad, especially as we are both Christmassy people who like to do Christmassy things together. So now I fly to her. After a festive English weekend in the countryside, with roaring fires, Sunday roast, and a certain amount of family madness, we always make sure to set off for London and lunch in the Wolseley.

In these past years, getting my mother out of the car, across two lanes of traffic, and through the grand doors does not go as speedily as it used to. First, there was choosing between the walking stick or the umbrella. Then it was the wind catching that formidable 1960s bouffant, which whooshed up and away—in order to settle it into place, she had to walk backward down Piccadilly.

After lunch we went to the Albany, London's oldest private residence, which comprises a set of apartments built more than two hundred years ago and has been home to prime ministers, poets, and film stars ever since. My parents had an apartment there for many years, and we had to be smuggled in as neither children, dogs, nor whistling were allowed.

OPPOSITE: All these flowers and berries were picked by David and me from our neighboring fields and lanes, and if you can believe it, I sewed them onto the edge of our burlap table runner so they would appear to be growing off the edges of the tables.

Tom
Geordie
Chris
Orlando

My brother inherited Albany when my mother decided she wanted to live in Oxfordshire full-time. As my brother is an artist, architect, designer, and aesthete, his "set," as the apartments are known, is ablaze with color and excitement, in stark contrast to some of his more monastic, straitlaced neighbors.

As we left the Albany, my mother stopped to shake hands with the top-hatted tailcoated porters whom she had known so well. "Nice to see you, milady," they said, just as the Fortnum & Mason clock across the street chimed three and broke the calm of that rarefied world. It was also my prompt to join a conference call with my team back in the States. "Where are you?" one of them asked. "Hard to explain," I said, looking back down the Albany's stone hallway, where women were only permitted after 1880. "I feel I've come a long way."

"Never let one meal interfere with another," said my mother firmly as we sat down to tea and chocolate cake in the Beaumont Hotel. My mother read the newspaper as I Skyped into a tricky meeting discussing forecasting figures. I felt a tap on my shoulder and took off my headphones. "Very good cake. There is jam in the middle," my mother said. She continued, "But what I really want are mince pies and brandy butter."

Welcome to the curious world of mince pies, a stalwart of the British Christmas. Claire—our Top Banana at home on Harbour Island—always wears her *God Save the Queen* apron when rustling up a batch in our kitchen. For the uninitiated, we should probably clear something up straight away: mince pies are not made of meat. That's just an insidious rumor, a bit like the one that Christmas crackers are for putting cheese on.

Well, all right, it's true that mince pies used to have meat in them. In the Middle Ages, Crusaders brought the first recipes back from the Middle East, and the British chucked in spices like nutmeg and cinnamon as a kind of naive homage to those far-flung lands. The pies then went through a series of eye-watering evolutions involving things like chopped tongue and mutton suet. The Tudors adored them, but they made the Puritans furious. Then again, everything made the Puritans furious.

The thing is, these innocuous-looking little numbers really divide the troops—some recoil at their mere mention, others cheer with festive joy. They pop up in early December and are finally put to bed around New Year's, by which time it's enough already.

But in the run-up to the big day, a lovingly arranged plateful, dusted with a light snow of icing sugar, cannot fail to fire up even the grinchiest Christmas soul. And while Father Christmas must be longing for British children to come up with some other welcome snack left by the fireplace on Christmas Eve, that's a tradition that isn't going anywhere. Mince pies are not for everyone, but hey, the Brits think pumpkin pie is weird. So long live the rather mad English traditions—including the completely meat-free and incredibly festive mince pie!

PAGES 188–189: Entertaining details: Chinese hat marquees, cucumber-covered salmon, fire pits, luggage label place settings, rolling pins, and local flowers. OPPOSITE: Top Banana's homemade mince pies involve a lot of icing sugar and sometimes a cut finger.

ABOVE AND OPPOSITE: Hints of the holidays: red-ribboned boxes, teatime with mince pies, my scented Black Hibiscus candle, and a roaring fireplace with crackers piled up in a Wedgwood vase. (An American friend once asked if there was cheese to go with the crackers.)

COUNTRY LIFE

Both Britwell House and the Grove are tucked between the two tiny towns of Wallingford and Watlington, between the villages of Ewelme, Brightwell Baldwin, and Britwell Salome. It is a convenient part of Oxfordshire, set in the rolling hills of the Cotswolds and only an hour from London.

I spent much of my childhood riding across acres and acres of its stubble fields, climbing apple trees, and collecting tadpoles.

My own children were christened in the Ewelme church, the same church I was christened in and where my father's funeral was held, although he insisted on being buried in the churchyard at Brightwell Baldwin, which he deemed much more stylish, much less squashed, and suitably opposite the Lord Nelson pub.

The Lord Nelson boasts a fine menu, two rooms to sleep in, roaring fires in winter, Pimm's in the summer, and year-round gossip from farmers and gentry alike, perched on barstools with snoozing dogs on the well-worn tartan carpet at their feet. A picture of the Queen hangs on the bar wall and Union Jacks swing from the low ceiling, reminding us we are British.

After my daughter Domino's christening in the church, we invited the throng of friends, family, and godparents across to the Lord Nelson. The children were held captive in the little town hall a few paces further down the lane, where a magician was meant to be keeping their attention. Although some of them, not to be named—Felix and Amory Flint Wood—climbed out of the bathroom window and ran back up to us in the pub.

OPPOSITE: The church at Brightwell Baldwin. My father lies peacefully here, shaded by beech trees and surrounded by his cherished English countryside.

OPPOSITE: Domino in 2008, with an appalling cold, dressed in the simple christening gown I had also been christened in, as had my sister and brother before me.
ABOVE: Inside the Brightwell Baldwin church that has hosted our family's christenings and funerals.

W
E

It's hard to imagine the English countryside without its churches. These are the places where visitors can find the echoes of previous ages—a place where the grand and the humble meet. I was recently given a beautifully bound book entitled *Early Colonists of the Bahamas*. The author had compiled the names of the early settlers, dating back to the 1700s, pulled from local church records. Without such records, there would no documentation of these names. Or of any names, be it in the Bahamas or Britain.

Every year until I was a teenager, Christmas was spent at Broadlands, my grandfather's home, and would begin with the traditional service of thanks in Romsey Abbey. We would sit in the family pew up by the high altar, close to the choir and the clergy. We would read from the prayer books that had filled this pew since 1810. And occasionally when we misbehaved, our nanny would take us tightly by the arm and remove us through the Norman side door that dated back to 1100. Inside the abbey, there is a memorial to my great-grandmother, and of course my grandfather lies there in a dark green marble tomb. My cousin Tim Knatchbull was married here. I'll never forget his ravishing bride, Isabella, stopping in front of the Queen as they walked down the aisle, bowing her head and dropping into the deepest and most dramatic of curtsies, the diamonds of the family tiara shimmering in the sunlight pouring in from the ancient glass windows. Unfortunately, I had missed the entire middle part of the service. Felix, then aged two, had decided that weddings were not his thing and began to scream at the top of his lungs. We had made a speedy exit, nipping back in for the closing hymn. At the reception afterward, the Queen looked at him, smartly dressed in his polished buckle shoes and linen shorts, and said, "He was well-behaved, wasn't he?"

The little church in Ewelme where I was christened was no less impressive; Geoffrey Chaucer's granddaughter is buried there. My mother is always amused by the fact that there is this marble figure of a very good-looking woman laid out on top of her tomb underneath which there is a casket of her bare bones. If you walk through the enormous oak doorway, down the ancient steps, and across into a courtyard, you will see the handsome almshouses dating from 1700 and still lived in today by worthy pensioners.

Toward the end of my father's life, he started to compile a small book which he titled *The Demise of David Hicks*. In this, he wrote out precise directions for how his funeral should be arranged, because Lord knows what his family might have organized if left without instructions. In the book, he clearly stated that his funeral service was to be held in the pretty church of Ewelme, but under no circumstance was he to be buried there—the main burial ground was all filled up, and the newly opened extension did not meet with the great designer's approval. Instead, he was to be laid to rest in the nearby village of Brightwell Baldwin. And so his coffin was carried from Ewelme, along the drive of the Grove, past the estate he had created, and to the graveyard of the church in Brightwell Baldwin, with the entire congregation in a snaking procession following behind. As my brother poetically put it, it was "the master leading a tour of his garden one last time."

PAGES 198–199: The distinguished Ewelme churchyard and the almshouses beyond. Little has changed in this scene for more than 600 years. Inside the church lies Geoffrey Chaucer's granddaughter, the Duchess of Suffolk. OPPOSITE: The Watlington town hall, built in 1664, has served as a market hall, school, court, and meeting room. Every Thursday, you can buy a jolly good piece of fish here or some local Oxfordshire honey.

One summer's day, I introduced my Argentinean friend Miguel to the area. I drove him first into the town of Watlington, where every Thursday a small crowd gathers under the arches of the red brick town hall to shop the local fare, which includes honey from busy Oxfordshire bees, seasonal flowers, fruit, and fish.

We lazily wandered down the high street, passing the family-owned butchers to the left, where straw boaters and pinstriped aprons are still worn, sheepskins line the windows, and enormous sausages hang from hooks.

Young mothers were lingering in the kitchen shop beyond, possibly buying a spatula, a gift card, or, in my case, huge wooden boards, earthy linen napkins, and raffia place mats.

The seductive smell of chocolate drifted in from the building next door, where two sisters have opened an artisanal handcrafted chocolate shop called Tutu Delicious. On one side of the building one sister, the chocolatier, will be creating her latest masterpiece, possibly pistachio, lavender, salt, or edible gold leaf, whilst on the other side of the building, the second sister is carefully serving customers. One feels like Alice, having fallen down a rabbit hole. Where on earth did these two magical maidens and their creations come from?

Next door to this orange-colored wonderland stands the Granary, a delicatessen with every possible type of cured meat, cheese, spice, and seed. Wooden crates hold local ales and ciders, including my favorite, the Village Idiot. Beautiful tall, triangular glass bottles with cork stoppers can be purchased and filled with homemade balsamic vinegar, which trickles out like syrup when a small tap is turned on a great urn. A candle burns in a brass candleholder, looking like something from a book of nursery rhymes. The owner explains that a candle has burned in the shop every day since it opened, the theory being that it helps digest the smell of cheeses. We buy a gigantic round of hard cheese: Saint Bartholomew, churned by Ian Fleming's granddaughter in the next village over.

In this confusing age of online shopping, the high street of Watlington holds a reassuring sense of countryside charm.

I drove Miguel to the top of Britwell Hill, noting proudly that "This is where Chitty Chitty Bang Bang takes off and flies." The hill was one of my earliest memories, of being pushed in my pram along the lane at the bottom. A few years later, I was watching my brother and sister race from the top on their bikes—when I pleaded to join them, my mother would say I was "much too young." I got my revenge years later when, with my own children, we stole my mother's salmon platter and used it as a sledge after a surprising snowstorm laid a thick blanket of white across the hill.

OPPOSITE: The Octagon House in our little village of Britwell Salome was conceived and designed by my father for an adventurous client.

PAGES 204–205: Wildflowers border the bridle way just beyond one of the farmhouses my father built. Note the H sign above the front door: Branding, branding, branding!
ABOVE: The Queen and Prince Philip watch over the comings and goings inside the pub. Unseen here but just above them are the words "Always time for a quickie" over a brass clock.
OPPOSITE: In the sleepy village of Brightwell Baldwin, the Lord Nelson Pub is never quiet. The landlord's dog can be seen most evenings balancing on a barstool as pints are pulled and pigeon is served.

SPECIALS
GRILLED SARDINES WITH GARLIC BUTTER
SCOLLOPS WITH BACON, SUN DRIED TOMATOES
MELON AND PARMA HAM 795
MONKFISH WITH ROASTED RED PEPPER DRESSING 1895
SKINNY FRIES + SALAD
ESCOLOPE OF VEAL, SAGE BUTTER SPINACH + SAUTE 1895
BEEF + PEPPER STIR FRY HOI SIN SAUCE + RICE 19.00
Baguettes – all served with skinny chips
Sausage + fried onion
Mature Cheddar + sticky onion chutney
Brie + avocado
Classic B. L. T All £8-95
Hot Beef
WiFi – c2666b683b
Sit back and allow us to attend to your every need whether it be a relaxing drink or a fab meal!

Passing through the village at the bottom, we stopped at the Red Lion shop, across the road from the Red Lion pub. On cold wintry nights Pat, my mother's beloved housekeeper, would sneak me into the pub so she could play darts on the evenings when I was left with her. I would leave with the smell of beer and tobacco infused into my school cardigan. Now the pub is a smart, small restaurant with the shop across the courtyard where a rather grand chap in a white coat and tie tells you the homemade pork pies have sold out and so have the sausage rolls, but you can buy a free-range chicken and they can just about tell you her name.

We drove past thatched cottages and stinky pig fields and across the little stone bridge of Wallingford to park in the town center and stroll through the antique arcade and smattering of shops. I bought a silver teapot with a wooden handle smooth from years of use. It cost less than £20, which made me sad for its forgotten time. A box of Legos would cost more.

We wandered down to the Tea & Coffee Company, where coffee is roasted and tea is blended, and bought a colossal bag of Earl Grey perfect for my teapot.

Later, we arrived on my mother's doorstep at the Grove, offering honey-combed chocolates and lemon drizzle cake, and meandered around the garden, created in geometric precision with allées of clipped hornbeam and secret rose gardens beside the folly my father built.

As the sun began to fade, we returned to my own home two fields away for a pre-dinner drink, the fragrance of the garden we had just toured—rose and peony petals, mown grass, and warm English rain—lingering in our memories.

OPPOSITE: After Domino's christening, we invited friends and family to cram into the pub. It was a freezing cold day, but roaring fires and a huge amount of mulled wine kept us warm.

LION FARM SHOP
FREE-RANGE CHICKENS FROM TRING
FAMOUS LEMON DRIZZLE CAKES

Saint Bartholomew
Unpasteurised, organic, hand-made, semi-hard cheese

OXFORDSHIRE

AGED MEAT
BEEF

BRANCH LIBRARY
Closed

£20

PAGES 210–211: Scenes from the surrounding towns. Life still ambles along at a gentle pace through this slice of England. OPPOSITE: Lady Hamilton presides over the dining room at the Lord Nelson. ABOVE: My overflowing treasure box and other pieces designed by me and hopefully loved by others.

OPPOSITE: Domino asked me what this was; I explained it was a telephone box where you put coins in and connected to a call. She looked amazed. ABOVE: Inside a local antiques store, where time really does stand still. PAGES 216–217: A slice of England.

POSTSCRIPT

In writing this book I have been able to wander back through the rooms of my past remembering moments, occasions, smells, and textures, all deeply rooted in the English countryside. And I have been able to share much of the present. I hope what comes across is the feeling of celebration and giving thanks. I am thankful for a life filled with friends, family, and a slice of England.

ACKNOWLEDGMENTS

This book is dedicated to my mother, and many of the acknowledgments must also be dedicated to her. She is a judge of great wit, wisdom, and humanity.

I bothered her a lot when compiling the first half of the book, asking about every house that had been her home: Broadlands, Britwell, and the Grove. Much of the time, I would sit beside her on the sofa and take notes as she reminded me that the "badges" on the senior staff's uniforms at the Viceroy's house were pinned, never sewn, or that the 7th Earl of Shaftesbury was my great-great-grandfather, not my great-grandfather.

Sometimes I would record us, but these recordings were normally unusable due to the rustling sounds of a chocolate box being opened and the rummaging through it to locate a rose cream.

Huge thanks to Miguel Flores-Vianna for photographing the book, which is our second one together. Miguel would arrive from some far-flung exotic location dapperly dressed in a tweed jacket ready for action and gentle gossiping. We do have fun. (And thanks to his two assistants, Brett Wood and Tim Smyth, for their infinite patience.)

Brittan Goetz has laid out the book, and she too is owed great thanks for all the twists and turns and endless annoying backseat driving from me. A few of her own images have slipped in, as she recorded much of this journey over the years.

My editor Kathleen Jayes allowed me to diverge from the script and include more personal anecdotes than Pantone colors in the copy. Thank you, Kathleen and Rizzoli.

Of course, my five kids and David have suffered the most. I was pretty much bat-shit crazy during a lot of this time, building a house and building a business, then running that business and writing this book. It's amazing they have stuck around.

CANDY

VILLAGE IDIOT

First published in the United States of America in 2018
by Rizzoli International Publications, Inc.
300 Park Avenue South
New York, NY 10010
www.rizzoliusa.com

PHOTO CREDITS:

All images © **MIGUEL FLORES-VIANNA** except: **INDIA HICKS**: Pages: 16, 20, 21, 92, 97, 134, 138, 178, 180, 181, 184, 185, 222, 223 **LADY PAMELA HICKS COLLECTION**: Pages: 14, 18 **DAVID HICKS ESTATE**: Pages: 24, 42, 43, 44, 55, 46, 48 **BRITTAN GOETZ**: Pages: 20, 90, 173, 190, 192, 193 **CHRISTIAN SINKINSON:** Pages: 187, 188, 189.

Text on pages 139 and 149 originally appeared in *Architectural Digest*. Text on pages 136-137 originally appeared in a slightly altered form in the *Daily Mail*.

2018 2019 2020 2021 / 10 9 8 7 6 5 4 3 2 1
Distributed in the U.S. trade by Random House, New York
Printed in China
ISBN-13: 978-0-8478-6177-4
Library of Congress Catalog Control Number: 2017957086

EARL MOUNTBATTEN OF BURM

QUEEN VICTORIA
1819-1901
m
PRINCE ALBERT
OF SAXE-COBURG
AND GOTHA
1819-1861

Victoria
Princess Royal
1840-1901
m
Emperor Frederick III
of Germany
1831-1888
(8 children)

King Edward VII
1841-1910
m
Princess Alexandra of Denmark
1844-1925

Princess Alice
1843-1878
m
Grand Duke Louis IV
of Hesse and the Rhine
1837-1892

Prince Alfred
Duke of Edinburgh
1844-1900
(1893 Duke of Saxe-Coburg and Gotha)
m
Grand Duchess Marie of Russia
1853-1920
(5 children)

Princess Helena
1846-1923
m
Prince Christian of
Schleswig-Holstein
1831-1917
(5 children)

King George V
1865-1936
m
Princess Mary of Teck
1867-1953

5 others

Princess Victoria of Hesse
1863-1950
m
Prince Louis of Battenberg
(1917 Marquess of Milford Haven)
1854-1921

Princess Elizabeth of Hesse
1864-1918
m
Grand Duke Serge of Russia
1857-1905

Princess Irene of Hesse
1866-1953
m
Prince Henry of Prussia
1862-1929
(3 children)

Grand Duke
Ernest Louis
of Hesse
1868-1937
m
Princess Eleonore
of Lich
1871-1937

Edward, Prince of Wales
1894-1972
(1936 King Edward VIII)
(1937 Duke of Windsor)
m
Wallis Simpson
1896-

King George VI
1895-1952
m
Lady Elizabeth Bowes Lyon
1900-

Princess Mary,
Princess Royal
1897-1965
m
6th Earl of Harewood
1882-1947
(2 children)

Henry,
Duke of Gloucester
1900-1974
m
Lady Alice Montagu-
Douglas-Scott
1901-
(2 children)

George, Duke of Kent
1902-1942
m
Princess Marina
of Greece
1906-1968
(3 children)

Princess Alice
1885-1969
m
Prince Andrew
of Greece
1882-1944

Princess Louise
1889-1965
m
King Gustaf VI
of Sweden
1882-1973

George,
2nd Marquess
of Milford Haven
1892-1938
m
Countess Nada
de Torby
1896-1963

EAR

E

Princess Elizabeth
1926-
(1952 Queen Elizabeth II)
m
Prince Philip
Duke of Edinburgh
1921-

Princess Margaret
1930-
m
Anthony Armstrong-Jones
Earl of Snowdon
1930-
(2 children)

Princess Cecile
1911-1937
m
Grand Duke George of Hesse
1906-1937
(3 children)

Princess Theodora
1906-1969
m
Margrave of Baden
1906-1963
(3 children)

Princess Margarita
1905-1981
m
Prince of Hohenlohe-
Langenburg
1897-1960
(5 children)

Princess Sophie
1914-
m
1. Prince Christopher
of Hesse Kassel
1901-1943
(5 children)
2. Prince George of Hanover
1915-
(3 children)

Prince Philip
Duke of Edinburgh
1921-
m
Princess Elizabeth
1926-
(1952 Queen
Elizabeth II)

Charles, Prince of Wales
1948-
m
Lady Diana Spencer
1961-

Princess Anne
1950-
m
Mark Phillips
1948-
(2 children)

Prince Andrew
1960-

Prince Edward
1964-

George, 4th Marquess
of Milford Haven
1961-

Lord Ivar
Mountbatten
1963-

Hon.
Norton Knatchbull
1947-
(1979 Lord Romsey)
m
Penelope Eastwood
1953-

Hon.
Michael-John
Knatchbull
1950-

Lady
Joanna Knatchbull
1955-
m
Baron Hubert
du Breuil
1956-

Prince William
1982-

Prince Henry
1984-

Hon.
Nicholas Knatchbull
1981-

Hon.
Alexandra Knatchbull
1982-